How Animals Hide

by Karen Latchana Kenney

1

Say hello to amicus readers.

You'll find our helpful dog, Amicus, chasing a ball—to let you know the reading level of a book.

Ⓐ

Learn to Read

Frequent repetition of sentence structures, high frequency words, and familiar topics provide ample support for brand new readers. Approximately 100 words.

Read Independently

Repetition is mixed with varied sentence structures and 6 to 8 content words per book are introduced with photo label and picture glossary supports. Approximately 150 words.

Read to Know More

These books feature a higher text load with additional nonfiction features such as more photos, time lines, and text divided into sections. Approximately 250 words.

Amicus Readers are published by Amicus
P.O. Box 1329, Mankato, Minnesota 56002

Series Editor   Rebecca Glaser
Book Editor   Wendy Dieker
Series Designer   Kia Adams
Book Designer   Heather Dreisbach
Photo Researcher   Heather Dreisbach

Printed in the United States of America at Corporate Graphics, in North Mankato, Minnesota.

1022
3-2011

10 9 8 7 6 5 4 3 2 1

Library of Congress Cataloging-in-Publication Data

Kenney, Karen Latchana.
    How animals hide / by Karen Latchana Kenney.
      p. cm. – (Amicus readers. Our animal world)
    Includes index.
    Summary: "A Level 1 Amicus Reader that describes how different animals hide from other animals by looking like their background, changing their physical appearance, and by altering their movement. Includes comprehension activity"– Provided by publisher.
    ISBN 978-1-60753-143-2 (library binding)
    1. Animals–Color–Juvenile literature. 2. Camouflage (Biology)–Juvenile literature. I. Title.
    QL767.K46 2011
    591.47'2–dc22

2010033475

Table of Contents

Look closely at this branch.
Do you see the stick bug?
It hides to keep safe from
other animals.

A katydid uses camouflage to hide. Its body looks like a leaf. On the ground, it moves under the trees.

A tawny frogmouth sleeps all day on a tree. It looks just like its background. Other animals do not notice this sleeping bird.

In winter, an arctic fox is hard to see. Its furry coat turns white. It blends with the snow.

Zebras stand closely together to hide. The pattern of their stripes tricks lions. They cannot pick one zebra from the group.

This octopus can copy
other animals. In the sea, it
changes shape and color.

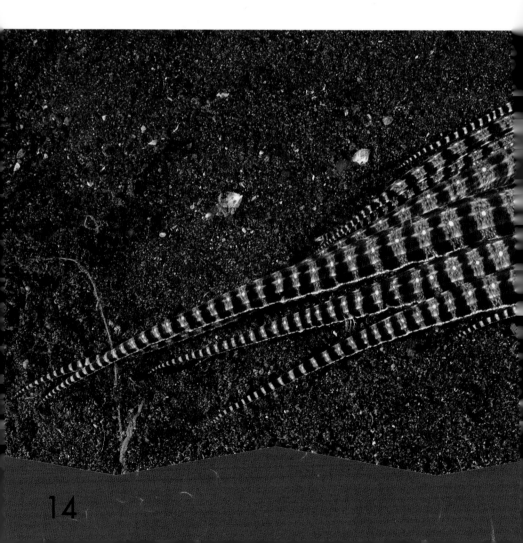

Looking like a deadly fish
keeps it safe.

copy
to do the same thing
or look the same as
something else

match
to be the same color
as another thing

pattern
the same colors and
shapes shown over
and over again

What Do You Remember?

Match each animal to what it looks like when it hides.

katydid

stick bug

deadly fish
pebbles
leaf
snow
tree
stick

arctic fox

octopus

tawny frogmouth

flounder fish

If you don't remember, read through the book again for the answers.

Ideas for Parents and Teachers

Our Animal World, an Amicus Readers Level 1 series, gives children fascinating facts about animals with ample reading support. In each book, a picture glossary reinforces new vocabulary. The activity encourages comprehension and critical thinking. Use the ideas below to help children get even more out of reading.

Before Reading

- Read the title of the book and show students the cover. Discuss the clues that the cover reveals about the book.
- Ask students to list ways they think animals hide. Write answers on the board.
- Look at the picture glossary. Discuss the meanings of the words.

During Reading

- Walk through the photos in the book. Ask: *What do the pictures show?* See if the students can spot the animals in the photos.
- Read the book aloud to students or have them read independently.
- After each spread, ask students to write the animal's name and what it looks like or does to hide.

After Reading

- Review the list students made before reading the book. Ask students to name other ways animals hide that they learned in the book.
- Use the What Do You Remember? activity on page 22 to help review the text.
- Discuss why students think hiding is an important skill for animals.

Index

Web Sites

American Museum of Natural History: OLogy
http://www.amnh.org/ology/

Click Magazine for Kids: Beatrice Looks at Animal Camouflage
http://www.clickmagkids.com/bworld/photos/beatrice-looks-animal-camouflage

University of Richmond WebUnit: Camouflage
http://chalk.richmond.edu/education/projects/webunits/adaptations/camou1.html